The Faith Conductor

Ursa O'Neill

Fountaingate Ministree

Author's Note;

Good day!! Welcome to a journey....an exploration of the word faith and what it means in our day to day life. This is a Journey Journal as there are quite a few pages left for you the reader to become the writer of your own story. This book is written from a Christian perspective and is based on the Bible, but also is a creative expression of my own feelings about faith. My hope is that you will find in these pages some inspiration to take time to contemplate your own faith, and that you will feel closer to God as a result.

I pray God you watch over the reader's passage through the passages of this book, that they find in the pages written or not yet written, gems of insight only You can give. Amen

Preface

Here is a story, a sermon, a loving preparation for you the reader. This little book has arisen out of a teaching about faith I prepared for my home church in March 2020. Our church had been suddenly told that we could no longer use the premises we had been meeting in for a couple of years prior. As I tried to imagine where I was going to deliver this message I pictured various venues in which it might take place. Little did I know it was to take place on Zoom, something I didn't have any knowledge of at the time of my imagining. As you may have guessed, this took place somewhere around the beginning of the first British covid lockdown. Featuring in this message is the imagery of a kite in flight, and as it happened just before I went to my bedroom to speak to my church online, I stepped out onto my roof terrace for some fresh air, just as I did this a few terraces away I could hear a man say "it takes a lot of wind to fly a kite". I knew this was confirmation that actually this was the best time and the best place to speak out this message. Now because of an inner prompting from

Holy Spirit, I feel to share this message with you…..

The Kite, The Key,
The Lightning Strike

F aith is like a frontier charted by our heart, the borders and the boundaries delineating a protective reflection on "what is". God *is*, faith sees this and seizes this reality, to take it in to a life lived within the vivid colours of the painted canvas of our life, that we are adorning with our understandings and expressions. God gives us the resources for creating our lives seemingly upon a fixed but empty canvas. Faith greatly affects what we choose to create and how faith works can feel a bit mysterious.

The Bible speaks much about faith and its importance as the very basis of our walk with God. Galatians 5:6 says;

"For in Christ Jesus neither circumcision nor uncircumcision counts for anything, but only faith working through love." (English Standard Version)

Though this passage is mainly addressing our right standing with God being based on faith, I also can't help but notice a clue about how faith works. In relationship to God our faith works through love! Love of God, love and care for people and ourselves. Also the scripture seems to portray that faith has a way of "working". I find faith a beautiful and many-faceted topic as it seems to have a wide range of meaning and application. Being a Christian, I believe the most important part of my faith is believing God is who He reveals himself to be in Bible. This faith ties us into a solid relationship with God where we can extend our love and listening first and foremost to Him, and then live out the expression of God's calling on our life. This book specifically addresses the part of faith that is about receiving from God, what He so dearly wants us to have, enjoy and give away……abundant Life !!!

Why is it that we can often feel our faith in our own life is not working to help us receive the loving things we hope for?……..things which God wants us to lay hold of. God's Word clearly indicates His good will and intention towards us and speaks promises to us of available blessings, that He wants us to have and actually experience. This little book is offered up as a creative and playful expression of how faith works in our life. This book is prepared as an exercise for you the reader to take time to ponder some of the aspects of your faith walk, and see how aligning with God's Word on any matter in your life can help to bring about the healing and help we need. This text aims to simply strengthen our trust in God and His Word to us. I have chosen quite a freestyle type of writing for this book and have left some space for you the reader to write about your own faith journey.

As I mentioned in the preface, this book began as a message for my home church. Holy Spirit seemed to deposit a picture of how faith works and at the moment I received this, I was filled with total peace and spent some time quietly pondering. The picture was this, the famous experiment of Benjamin Franklin in which he sought to prove that lightning was indeed electrical. In the experiment Franklin constructed a kite with a wire at the top, the kite was attached to a hemp string with a metal house key attached near the bottom, he fixed a silk rope in order to insulate, that would stay dry so he could hold the kite safely from within the doorway of a shed. On a stormy day in Philadelphia, Franklin and his son conducted this experiment, they launched the kite flying within the ambient electrical charge of the storm. History was made as they conducted an electrical charge from the air, through the wire, along the wet hemp string to the key and then carefully attracting electricity towards Franklin's lifted fist—a shocking success. It is important to note that lightning didn't strike Mr Franklin's kite but that the electric charge present was enough to draw electricity from the heavens.[12]

Franklin described the event this way in a statement he made for an article from the Philadelphia Gazette, on October 19th 1752;

"As soon as any of the Thunder Clouds come over the Kite, the pointed Wire will draw the Electric Fire from them, and the Kite, with all the Twine, will be electrified, and the loose Filaments of the Twine will stand out every Way, and be attracted by an approaching Finger. And when the Rain has wet the Kite and Twine, so that it can conduct the Electric Fire freely, you will find it stream out plentifully from the Key on the Approach of your Knuckle."[3]

Franklin went on to explain he could capture this charge into a specially prepared phial (a glass jar for experiments) from the key on the kite string. As he stated within the same article noted above, this experiment demonstrated "the sameness of electric matter with that of lightning".

This story contains clear imagery that can be related to different aspects of faith which contribute to how we receive God's precious promises into our hands and into our lives. This book lays out 6 aspects of faith, symbolically using the components of this experiment to express, how our faith enables us to receive from God, so that we can give from God to take care of the needs of ourselves and the people we encounter. This book also invites you the reader to try this experiment at home in a symbolic way, in order to refresh and invigorate your faith.

Hebrews 11:6 ; "But without faith it is impossible to please Him, for he who comes to God must believe that He is, and that He is a rewarder of those who diligently seek Him." (New King James Version)

Here is some space to reflect in writing on how faith fits into your life at the moment. Is it working? Are you comforted by the nearness of God and seeing signs of Him in your life and able to follow His leading? You can take time just to rest and relate to God and see what inspiration comes while you write…

1. National Archives, under the heading Founder's online, with title The Kite Experiment, 19 October 1752.[https://founders.archives.gov/documents/Franklin/01-04-02-0135]Some of the general information about how this experiment was conducted, included in my book, was gleaned from "Priestley's Account" which is a document that features website noted above.

2. Some of the general info about Franklin's Kite experiment was gleaned from a website called The Franklin Institute from this specific page called Benjamin Franklin and the Kite Experiment; https://www.fie.edu/en/science-and-education/benjamin-franklin/kite-key-experiment2023

3. All Quotes from Franklin's Statement published in the Philadelphia Gazette are found on a website called National Archives, under the heading Founder's online, with title The Kite Experiment, 19 October 1752. [https://founders.archives.gov/documents/Franklin/01-04-02-0135]

Walk

Walk on out into the storm. Benjamin Franklin and his son walked to a field where the storm was active to go to a suitable place to conduct their experiment. [1] Most of us have found ourselves in one type of storm or another metaphorically, we have needs, wishes, desires, various circumstances to navigate. In God we do not need to back down if He is calling us forward, calling us to receive what we need, and making plain and evident to us His promises within His word. We need to walk without fear where God is calling us….to a place of active and aware engagement with Him….to a place where our faith rises up sensing His power and love. Our footsteps moving forward propelling us deeper within God's majesty, power and grace. There is always passion and purpose and when aligned with His Spirit they work together so well. So even if the emotions feel a bit messy, know that they are similar to the force that keeps bringing in the tide of the sea always on time ! Stormy seas need not deter!

Matthew14:24-14:31 "….But the ship was now in the midst of the sea, tossed with waves: for the wind was contrary. And in the fourth watch of the night Jesus went unto them walking on the sea, they were troubled saying, It is a spirit; and they cried out for fear. But straightway Jesus spake unto them, saying, Be of Good cheer; it is I; be not afraid. And Peter answered Him and said, Lord if it be thou, bid me come unto thee on the water. And he said, Come. And when Peter was come down out of the ship, he walked on the water to go to Jesus. But when he saw the wind boisterous; he was afraid and beginning to sink , he cried, saying, Lord, save me. And immediately Jesus stretched forth his hand, and caught him, and said unto him, O thou of little faith, wherefore didst thou doubt?" (King James Version).

Mark 6:48 "Seeing them straining at the oars—for the wind was against them—at about the fourth watch of the night, He came to them walking on the sea; and He intended to pass by them." (New American Standard Bible)

I have often been inspired by this story because of how vividly it speaks of our own walk of faith. Stepping out toward Jesus, walking on the water a little way, but then becoming distracted or impressed by things "contrary" and beginning to sink…..but even then Jesus is immediately ready to rescue and point out what can help us go further on in faith. Doubt out, and faith in! There is a hint in this story too which evokes the feeling that we need to take some action on our part, in communicating with the Lord and following His example of how He operates in faith…."He intended to pass by them". Call out to Him, reach out to Him, walk to Him with unwavering focus upon Him!

We are not getting anywhere in this example of faith….until we start moving. Holding nothing but the simplicity of a child's toy we move forward, walking upon the path God has for us.

Here is some space to write out some feelings if you wish, about what you are going through, what you are hoping for and how you feel God is calling you, instructing you, or delivering you, in whatever you are facing in life right now. Psalm 34:19 (New King James Version) "Many are the afflictions of the righteous, but the Lord delivers him out of them all"…..

1. National Archives, under the heading Founder's online, with title The Kite Experiment, 19 October 1752.[https://founders.archives.gov/documents/ Franklin/01-04-02-0135]Some of the general information about how this experiment was conducted, included in my book, was gleaned from "Priestley's Account" which is a document that features on website noted above.

The Wire

God's whole being is one of total goodness. His goodness overflows and the Word makes clear that God desires us to receive fully of his goodness to fill up our own lives so that we can in turn bless those around us in manifold ways. God's Word is His Truth in print, for all to view. The Word is the basis for every wish of the Father to emerge from his heart into our earth and beyond. We can sometimes think God's will is secret, but much of it is in plain sight given unreservedly as a guideline for us to follow in the Bible. The Wire represents the undeniable Truth which is without compromise or manipulation. The wire stands as pure substance ready to transmit the power of God. I welcome you to try it, find a scripture you want to see more of in your life…set it up at the top of your kite and watch it glow!

First things first! God is always first, paramount, unparalleled in our love, attention and affection! Turning to Him in worship can cause even the most difficult of circumstances to quickly unravel and become a chain broken, a prisoner now free. Countless extreme moments of wonder have occurred for me when engaging in worshipping God; communion with God, visions, warm Presence filled dance, insight and instruction, enjoyment of others within the Church. I remember one notable time when I was struggling to wholeheartedly forgive someone. After attending a worship evening my whole heart attitude towards the person had without any effort on my part completely transformed into a positive loving attitude ! I did nothing to change! I just worshipped God. Choosing God above all else, is a heart choice and also the 1st commandment !

A heart set on Him will always come back to valuing Him more than any detail of our existence. However part of loving God is respecting and honouring His wishes, and God clearly shows in His Word that He wishes us to prosper in every are of life and to build up our life with our obedient faith. A part of worshipping God is actively believing and acting upon His Word.....taking Him at His Word, trusting His expression and choice.

For the exercise of this small book I would like to choose a request Moses made to God in Exodus 33:18 "Please show me Your Glory" (New King James Version). I believe prayers made in the Bible can be an invitation for us to pray in a similar manner. God responds to Moses in Exodus 33:19 "I will make all My goodness pass before you and I will call out my name Yahweh, before you." (New Living Translation). I don't know which way God will choose to show "me" His glory but I am excited to find out! So while you the reader observe, I am placing this as the wire that I will attach to my symbolic Kite. You can choose your own scripture, scriptural principle or scriptural promise to be your wire....let's see what happens in this exciting electric experiment!!

Here is some space to describe what the wire in your personal experiment is. I think for this it is important to stick with a scripture or clear scriptural principle so that we know we are aligning ourselves with God's will for our life. Perhaps a scripture around health, peace, provision, protection or anything you feel God calling you to choose.

Wait on Him.....He beckons....He indicates....He speaks to us....praise be to God. Turning our affections to Him in worship brings so much clarity and health into our lives!

The Kite Upon The Wind

L et go and Launch
  Learn from the indications of the wind and
  quality of air,
to know where to launch this kite,
Walk on out....
launch your wishes upon the wind.

One of the reasons Benjamin Franklin was so excited about his experiment was because it was simple to conduct. Here are his instructions to do with the construction of the kite.[1]

"Make a small Cross of two light Strips of Cedar, the Arms so long as to reach to the four Corners of a large thin Silk Handkerchief when extended; tie the Corners of the Handkerchief to the Extremities of the Cross, so you have the Body of a Kite; which being properly accommodated with a Tail, Loop and String, will rise in the Air, like those made of Paper; but this being of Silk is fitter to bear the Wet and Wind of a Thunder Gust without tearing." (From

Franklin's statement written up in the Philadelphia Gazette October 19th 1752)
This is a longer chapter….there is a lot to cover within the four corners of this handkerchief.

For our experiment the construction of the kite, is in acknowledging and utilising biblical principles. Applying trust in God and His Word is conducive to the flow of faith in our life. There is a method of dream interpretation which Carl Jung brought forward where everyone and everything in the dream represents you in some way. This exercise reminds me of that a bit, although this dynamic symbol of faith we are making, cannot exist without the very real presence of God. In this picture I see the wind as Holy Spirit and the kite as our full trust. Let yourself be carried!

The Holy Spirit helps us, He lifts our fragile frame by His grace overflowing, billowing with blasts of heavenly wind taking us higher as we lean and lay our fabric of trust on God's very essence, who holds and carries us, surrounds us and imbues us with His own power working in us, to produce His own desired outcomes….. and out they come!

We can absolutely trust God, His whole initiative is complete goodness and He is the expert on what goodness is! Think of the central prayer Jesus instructs His followers to pray;

Matthew 6:10-13;
"Our Father in heaven,
Hallowed be Your name.
Your kingdom come.
Your will be done
On earth as it is in heaven.
Give us this day our daily bread.
And forgive us our debts,
As we forgive our debtors.
And do not lead us into temptation,
But deliver us from the evil one.
For Yours is the kingdom and the power
and the glory forever. Amen"
(New King James Bible)

God's will for every good outcome to take place is clearly evident in this prayer, and also shows the attitude we need, while we knit ourselves closer to Him in practice day by day. Invest in today!! This is another day you have been given to draw closer to God, and think, move and act for Him. Add to this equation, the reality that this central guided prayer which Jesus instructs us to pray....and the basis of all prayer....can be coupled with Mark 11:24;

"Therefore I say to you, all things
for which you pray and ask,
believe that you have received them
and they will be *granted* to you."
(New American Standard Bible)

Is that not heartening news ! On earth as it is in heaven received !!! Received by us through Jesus, because of His wonderful good will towards us !!! So then........

Lying back on the wind I let myself lift and fly, leaning into the sureness of God's promises, His response and fulfilment of prayers, His response to me, someone He loves the way He loves Jesus, His sovereign goodness, and how He guides me to give, leaning back in total trust of the one who really knows what He is talking about.

Do you feel sometimes we as humans revert back to following unintentionally a perspective that we guess must be wisdom even though it doesn't line up with what God actually says? As we lean back on the wind and lift up, we let our perspective widen and understand more of the truth. Avoiding getting caught up in the entanglement of fear, God instructs us to throw fear out, but even so oftentimes we can get reeled in, hooked in, sunk, into the trembling over one thing or another. Really the only one we are instructed to fear is God Himself. When you plug every last bit of your fearing capacity into God….the act of fearing suddenly becomes a channel for Love, health and nurturing that arises within you. And what to do with fear if it does come up? A major practice that has turned my life around has been learning to just give all my difficulty to God.

1 Peter 5:7
"Throw the whole of your anxiety upon Him, because He Himself cares for you" (Weymouth New Testament).

I ask God to help me with this process and He does! We know He declares Himself to be our "helper" over and over in His Word, helping us through every thing we encounter in our life and being right there with us through it all. Fear also diminishes when we establish that our whole priority in life is God, thus showing that we "fear" Him. What are we really in this for? For us??? Or for Him?? Jesus is very strong on this matter and understanding this can be a most freeing thing within our Christian walk and life!

Luke 14:26;
"If anyone comes to Me and does not hate his father and mother, wife and children, brothers and sisters, yes, and his own life also, he cannot be My disciple." (New King James Version)

Understanding then that we can let go of every aspect of our life and simply learn from Him and follow Him in all aspects of our life, frees us up to move forward with Him and relate with Him, and give from Him. This is the truest desire of our heart, being in unity with God.

And also on His end what a gift he has given us, and

what a heart He has towards us……

Isaiah 43:25;
"I—I am He who is blotting out Thy transgressions for Mine own sake, And thy sins I do not remember." (Young's Literal Translation)

2 Corinthians 1:20
"For all the promises of God in Him are Yes, and in Him Amen, to the glory of God through us." (New King James Version)

God's intentions for us are always truly, truly good, even if for a time we endure very hard things. He will carry us…..through.

The more we trust, the more we fly!
The material of the kite is quite delicate, but that delicateness is essential to be lifted up on the wind. We need to be light, and we need to be sensitive and obedient to the Holy Spirit. We may need to let go of a few things to catch a hold of that lightness within us.

Coming back to the experiment I am doing as I write this book, I have been leaning into and relying on the truth that Jesus expects me to believe I have the answers to the prayers which are in line with Him….a direct line to His heart. The Kite is becoming more and more lofty in its point of view as it is lifted by the hand of the wind, held up by Holy Spirit. Rising to a new perspective which is able to grasp more of the detail involved in the truth we experience....a gift from Him. The material of this kite Benjamin Franklin used is silk, shiny, soft, smooth, delicate but strategic in its objective to be carried upwards. Deal with any doubt! You may need to ask The Lord to help you let go of any ideas causing you to doubt, The Lord wants to bring about your request. Keep going back to His Word, keep letting go of all else and holding on to God. Interesting how it is precisely this light delicateness, vulnerability and humility, that enables connection with God to take place at all. Leaning now on His view, His way of perceiving and framing the world in front of us, we are carried upwards to find His power working.

Explain how the idea of being the kite feels like to you. How does letting go of fear and doubt and lightening up, apply in your circumstance? How will trusting and relying on God fully, whilst acknowledging some of one's own frailty, effect change in your personal sense of peace and freedom?....and what about the sheer joy of flying !!!
1. Information on a website called National Archives, under the heading Founder's online, with title The Kite Experiment, 19 October 1752. This was from Franklin's Statement published in the Philadelphia Gazette 1752[https://

founders.archives.gov/documents/
Franklin/01-04-02-0135]

Holy Spirit Wind

H oly Spirit Wind;

….He is the like the wind, the animator, the movement and momentum of our communion with God….He is the very Life of God breathing our own story to life and holding us up.

In the Old Testament writings the word for spirit is Ruach and can mean breath, wind and spirit.[1] Similarly
in the New Testament, the word for spirit "Pneuma"[2], indicates wind, spirit and breath.

Jesus Himself likens the Spirit with the wind saying in **John 3:8;**

"The wind blows where it wishes,
and you hear the sound of it,
but cannot tell where it comes from
and where it goes.

So is everyone who is born of the Spirit"

(New King James Version)

The Holy Spirit is our help and source, carrying us and depositing us into connection with God. We can get pretty excited about the electricity in this experiment but how important is the wind in bringing this all together, keeping our humble fabric and frame up, and bringing about connection with God. The wind of the Holy Spirit can feel unpredictable but is always good. We need to hold the kite and cast it to the wind, throw the net out to catch the fish, lower the bucket to draw the water. Drawing on what is already given, we retrieve all we need and as well enough to give away. It is important to note that the Holy Spirit is resident in us and that we are joined to the Lord as "one spirit with Him" (1 Corinthians 6:17 New King James Version) …….so although we are relating to God in this high flying faith metaphor we are building, the story is happening somewhere within us where we are already held in unity with God.

Find time in reflection to wait, wonder, sigh, breathe the fresh air of freedom held in your union with the Holy Spirit who is in you. Write what you feel about your relationship to The Holy Spirit and how He is holding up your humble frame and connecting you to God's power and promise.

1. Strong's Exhaustive Concordance, 7307 ruach, https://biblehub.com/strongs/hebrew/7307.htm

2. Strong's Exhaustive Concordance, 4151. pneuma, https://biblehub.com/strongs/greek/4151.htm

The Rope

Hold on!! Twisting in our fingers is "The Rope", the rope once woven, we now hold on to. I can hear the rope tightening in the approaching lightning. The hairs of the fibres will begin to stand on end, but before that we just hold on. The rope is all about just holding on! Holding on keeps our conscious connection with God, as we hold onto His promises, trusting in His goodness;

"But those who wait on the Lord
Shall renew *their* strength;
They shall mount up with wings like eagles,
They shall run and not be weary,
They shall walk and not faint."
(Isaiah 40:31 New King James Version)

Hold sturdy have hope! Waiting can feel uncomfortable, we may feel we are being stretched, but it is one of the best parts of relating to God, being held in His strength and comfort while we wait and look to Him. Letting go of all else to hold onto

Him. Hold onto that one rope that leads directly to communion with God. If God says that Trusting, Hoping and having Faith are a good plan….than they most certainly are!

Things can get very tough in the wait….feeling tangled and tight…

…..or there can be such beauty of connection, holding on to the One we trust and knowing He is holding us. Keep following his direction at every turn. Hope keeps us tied to God even when everything else in our life feels like it is falling away.

The first mention of the Hebrew word for hope in scripture is really interesting to note. The Hebrew word "Tiqvah"[1] means hope and expectation but it also means cord and comes from the word qavah. Qavah means; gather together, look, patiently, wait for or wait upon and comes from a primitive root that alludes to the twisting together it takes to make a strong cord (Strong's Exhaustive Concordance 6960). Qavah is the word "wait" in the scripture quoted above… "those who wait on the Lord". Tiqvah is the word used for rope which appears in Joshua 2:18, referred to as a scarlet rope which Rahab used to help lower the spies to safety from the wall of Jericho. The same rope that she was instructed by the spies to lower so that her and her household would be spared on the day of battle. I can't help seeing some beautiful symbolism in the colour of this rope reminiscent of the blood on the doorposts at Passover and the blood of our Lord Jesus that sanctifies and saves us. We really do have something to hold onto that will rescue us entirely.

I can feel the building of momentum of receiving the promises of God, the hairs of the rope are standing on end, the air is electric with anticipation. The wind of the Holy Spirit is still holding this kite up and all that is really ours to do is to hold on !!! Just hold on to the promises as the emotions mount and the accounting of the mind creates a sum of loss….hold on….hold to God….hold on through. God has a plan, He is capable, He has given us *everything* to see His own desire through….and His own desire is you…all of you, your ways and your days and each glance you take towards him in thought or deed, He sees!

Hold on to that rope, the best is yet to come!!!

Here is some space to write how holding onto God has felt for you. What has caused hope to be stirred up in you? What has inspired you not to give up on expecting God's goodness, even when things are really tough? Do you feel securely attached to God? However long this waiting goes on for, where are you?…..and where is God?…..knowing He will never leave you….no doubt He is right there with you…..

1. Strong's Exhaustive Concordance, 8615. tiqvah as found on internet website Bible Hub specifically for this https://bilehub.com/strongs/

hebrew/8615.htm

The Key

A hh... can you feel it? The key is a little more substantial than the rope. Now we are getting somewhere! This key represents the deposit of faith God himself has placed in us, and it is the same substance as the wire at the top of the kite that is like a rod to God, His truth in His words, it is a gift and we have it, and we do well to acknowledge it. A key doesn't unlock things on it's own though, we've got to grab a hold of it and place it in the right lock...where it fits every time. The edges are intricately shaped with precision to meet the demand of the protection of the treasure. It's a divine set up...that God calls us to engage in. Taking initiative to trust and be confident that God wants His promises fulfilled for us more than we do! Rest in trust, lean on God...He is about to act.....

"Now faith is the substance of things hoped for, the evidence of things not seen."
(Hebrews 11:1 New King James Version)

Really lining up our belief to what is expressed in the word of God is very key......lining up our mind with the Truth. Remember the link between what we believe and what we receive. I believe God has given us faith, but also that there is a choosing and creating and a growing in faith that is up to us. When we agree with God's word on a matter we are really saying "yes" to God's perspective and He responds to our free will.....and waits for us to choose. It's true we are in a process of being shaped by God and our path through life is not so easy, but God is not holding out on us!

"He who did not spare His own Son, but delivered Him up for us all, how shall He not with Him also freely give us all things?"
(Romans 8:32 New King James Version)

A key in believing for God's promises to be evident in our lives, is the knowledge that God has cleared and cleansed us through the sacrifice of Jesus. It would be hard to trust we had much good coming our way if we felt there was some sort of barrier between us and God. The New Testament makes it abundantly clear that any barrier between us and God has been entirely done away with, when we place our trust in Jesus.

"For by one offering He has perfected forever those who are being sanctified"
(Hebrews 10:14 New King James Version)

When we know we are made clean and perfected by Him, we know there is no barrier to God's goodness flowing into every area of our life. I have been blessed with a vision from God that made this really clear to me. I was attending an evening at a small countryside church in England where Rolland Baker was preaching with great freedom and insight. During the songs of worship God said to me "speak to me about your shame". I wasn't aware that I had any issues about shame but I thought to myself I better do as He says because it's God telling me to do this. I spoke to God about my shame and the next thing that happened is I had a strong inner vision of God's face and then my attention was drawn to His eye and His eye was looking at Jesus. Jesus was in a spot light and looked absolutely perfect in every way; His robes, His beauty and His whole way. I was stunned by His perfection. Then my attention was drawn to God's eye again and I saw Him looking at me, and I was perfect, I was totally perfect in His sight just like Jesus. Obviously seeing myself in that light was surprising but God was sharing with me His view! I remember thinking, "what was I thinking? how did I think I could add to what Jesus has already done". I was seeing that my works were not going to bring about my perfection….only Jesus can. Instantly a song came to me with these words "I've put on Your righteousness, you just can't get better than that!" As you can see this vision made me experience first hand what was quoted in the scripture above "…He has perfected forever those who are being sanctified." This scripture has often intrigued me with the balance of having been perfected but being sanctified, which seems to speak about the process we can still see going on in our very real development.

"Christ has redeemed us from the curse of the law, having become a curse for us (for it is written "cursed is everyone who hangs on a tree") that the blessing of Abraham might come upon the Gentiles in Christ Jesus, that we might receive the promise of the Spirit through faith." (Galatians 3:13 & 14, New King James Version)

Having been cleared and cleansed we know we can await the wonder of God's goodness in our lives, even His own Spirit dwelling in us.

It is also key to know our authority in Christ, Jesus says;
"Behold, I give you authority to trample on serpents and scorpions, and over all the power of the enemy, and nothing shall by any means hurt you."(Luke 10:19 New King James Version)

We hold a blessing of being able to take creative action that is aligned with God. Nothing can stop us....but ourselves. Take up your authority, turn the key, open the door, there is more.....

Here is some space to write out your own sense of

the faith key God has placed in your hand. Are you able to count promises in God's word as real and applicable to you? Are you worried about anything getting in the way? Spend some time celebrating what God really has done for you in rescuing you and restoring you. Whatever you chose for your wire, write about how you see the signs coming together for these good things to take place in your life.......and that is the key.

The Hand

R each out your hand.

"And when the rain has wet the Kite and Twine, so that it can conduct the Electric Fire freely, you will find it stream out plentifully from the Key on the Approach of your Knuckle."[1]

There is a time when we can't mess around anymore but need to take action on something. If someone offers you some food when you are a guest in their home (and you want it) you will indeed take it, you will not wait till the host places it in your mouth! Jesus talks about this kind of thing when He instructs us to "believe that you have received" (Mark 11:24 as quoted earlier). That word "received" in the Greek comes from the word "lambano"[2]which is defined in Strong's Exhaustive Concordance as "to take, receive" and describes that the word specifically indicates "to get hold of" and that it is an active word. In this faith metaphor detailed in this book Benjamin Franklin lifts his hand near to the key to observe "Electric

Fire" being drawn to his hand. How do we take action on believing we have received? I would say that is something we find out for ourselves in our engagement with God. I think we need to actively trust and show trust of God and the Truth He details in His word, listening also carefully for His specific prompting to us. Whatever the matter, although God wants us to wait on Him, and trust in Him, and hope in Him, He does call us to believe in things before we see them....similar to what He does when He speaks creation into being.

Romans 4:17
"....the God who gives life to the dead and calls into being what does not yet exist."
(Berean Standard Bible)

Taking a look at taking, in faith;
I will give an example of believing you have received. The subject of this example may be appropriate to the promise you are believing for, if you have chosen a promise of Health in your experiment. I love this understanding and firm foundation for knowing that God has given us a promise of healing. Looking first to Isaiah 53:4;

"Surely our sicknesses he hath borne, And our pains —he hath carried them, And we—we have esteemed him plagued, Smitten of God, and afflicted."(Young's Literal Translation)

Isaiah 53 is a prophetic description of the crucifixion of Jesus and what it means for us. Many Christians believe healing is included in this atonement and one of the many ways we can believe in God's promise to make healing available to us. I'm slowly getting to a point here. There has been some debate over how to translate the words in the text above "sicknesses" and "pains", though literally this is what they are, many translations choose "griefs" and "sorrows" instead. But I think scripture is often the best interpreter of itself, in Matthew 8:17 it is written;

"This happened so that what was spoken through Isaiah the prophet would be fulfilled: HE HIMSELF TOOK OUR ILLNESSES AND CARRIED AWAY OUR DISEASES." (New American Standard Bible)

Amen!!! Taking a special look at that word "TOOK" it is again from the word "lambano"; "take,receive" as mentioned earlier. If Jesus calls us to believe we have received, it is not just a standing by and waiting kind of received because the word used denotes an action and is compared with Jesus taking our illnesses upon Himself on the cross which was complete and successful!! He took our sicknesses and wants us to take His Health....into every area of our life!

Also I am saying this "believing" will cause us to take actions in line with what we believe, closely listening to Him for what is appropriate in our situation. In one man's situation recorded in the Bible this story went as follows in Matthew 12:13 where Jesus was in the middle of healing a man with a withered hand.

"Then He said to the man, "Stretch out your hand". And he stretched it out and it was restored as whole as the other" (New King James Version)

In this man's case reaching for his healing meant just reaching out his hand.... and there was the healing in the midst of the obedience. It takes trust to obey God and agree with what He declares to be true in His word, and to believe we have received when we have asked and prayed for His promises to become our reality.

So "stretch out your hand" can you feel the approaching electrical charge at your finger tips. Yes right here within our reach, all the good things God wants us to receive.

Psalm 34:10;
"The young lions lack and suffer hunger; But those who seek the LORD shall not lack any good thing." (New King James Version)

Here is some space to write out what lifting your hand to the approaching electrical charge means to you...what steering your thoughts towards the words of God and receiving true revelation of what is actually real, feels like to you. What does it feel like to believe before you see? Within the subject you have chosen in your "kite experiment" what do you hear God calling you to do?

1. All Quotes from the Philadelphia Gazette are found on a website called National Archives, under the heading Founder's online, with title The Kite Experiment, 19 October 1752.[https://founders.archives.gov/documents/Franklin/01-04-02-0135]

2. Strong's Exhaustive Concordance, 2983 lambano, https://biblehub.com/strongs/greek/2983.htm

The Jar

R ight, what have we got?

"At this key the Phial may be charg'd; and from Electric Fire thus obtain'd, which are usually done by the Help of a rubbed Glass Globe or Tube; and thereby the Sameness of the Electric Matter with that of Lightning compleatly demonstrated."[1]

We have arrived at the end of this experiment....no loose ends here just a jar to hold all these wonderful realities and gifts in...the gifts of the Kingdom of God manifest. We store up a deep treasure; given out of a great reservoir of love that stretches back to before the stars were lit aglow and goes forward forever without ceasing.

James 1:17 (New King James Version);
"Every good gift and every perfect gift is from above, and comes down from the Father of lights, with

whom there is no variation or shadow of turning."
Romans 5:5 (New King James Version);
"Now hope does not disappoint, because the love of God has been poured out in our hearts by the Holy Spirit who has been given to us"

Now there is no more we could wish for than this, God's love poured out….and the Holy Spirit given. What an incredible reality we have! Within this out-pouring we have received there also many outcomes that happen because of it….some have already happened some waiting to happen. There is purpose in the release of God's Spirit to us and things God desires to see through us engaging with Him. If we are meant to do the work's of Jesus as well as greater works as He says, we are going to need all that God wants to grace us with.

John 14:12
"Most assuredly, I say to you, he who believes in Me, the works that I do he will do also; and greater *works* than these he will do, because I go to My Father." (New King James Version)

2 Corinthians 9:8
"And God *is* able to make all grace abound toward you, that you, always having all sufficiency in all *things*, may have an abundance for every good work."(New King James Version)

Ephesians 3:14-

"For this reason I bow my knees to the Father of our Lord Jesus Christ, from whom the whole family in heaven and earth is named, that He would grant you, according to the riches of His glory, to be strengthened with might through His Spirit in the inner man, that Christ may dwell in your hearts through faith; that you, being rooted and grounded in love, may be able to comprehend with all the saints what is the width and length and depth and height— to know the love of Christ which passes knowledge; that you may be filled with all the fullness of God." (New King James Version)

What ?? Filled with all the fullness of God! This being a prayer….and a prayer from the Bible…we know we can believe we've got this fullness even before we see the results! Faith is active in the journey to visible fulfilment of prayer.

I was blessed with a lovely happening which helped me to believe I had received the fullness of God into myself. I was resting my head on my husband's pillow and I felt to ask God to confirm two things for me; that my mustard seed of faith in Jesus had grown into a mustard tree that was at least taller than the moon and that God really had given me all that He has. The first request was acknowledging that my faith in Jesus did need to go on growing, but hoping that it at least stretched to over the moon….and I am over the moon with how amazing God is, as you can probably tell by now. The second request was in response to many scriptures which speak of God in-dwelling us in a very complete and real fashion. Other scriptures give a sentiment that we have been vey much included into God and all He has, specifically for His purposes.

Psalm 16:5&6 (New King James Version)
"O Lord, You are the portion of my inheritance and my cup; You maintain my lot. The lines have fallen to me in pleasant places; Yes I have a good inheritance."

So in my own outlandish way I was asking God if I really can believe I have all He has. As I rested my head on my husband's pillow with these two questions in mind, I said to God "if these things are true then come into my life the image of the moon in a jar" and I said "this will kill two birds with one stone"....then I said "No, don't kill any birds for this!" It is important to note that my husband was in another city at this time and could not have heard me! About 10 days later (which has often been the response time on my prayers if they are asking for a sign) above a bench in the hall I had designated for prayer was hung an incredibly beautiful picture. In the centre of the picture is a bird flying high (very much alive) in the night sky over the tree tops, and with it's beak holding onto a jar with the moon in it!!! I examined it for a while until I realised what had taken place. Then as if I needed further confirmation the next new picture in the hall was all about the phases of the moon and how it is illuminated by the sun. As you may have guessed my husband purchased and hung these pictures without any knowledge of my prayers.

Experiences like these encourage me to go further into finding out the true wonder God has placed us in when He transferred us into His Kingdom and the true wonder we now hold within.

"For God, who said, "Let light shine out of darkness," made his light shine in our hearts to give us the light of the knowledge of God's glory displayed in the face of Christ. But we have this treasure in jars of clay to show that this all-surpassing power is from God and not from us." (2 Corinthians 4:6&7 New International Version)

As a believer it is like we always stand within this ambient electrical charge, always ready to transmit the love and power of God, look around, He is active in your life!

I have experienced many wonderful answers to prayer as well as having to just hope and wait and trust without seeing all the results I had hoped for. Through all of it, I have perceived the Spirit of God helping me, teaching me, guiding me and reassuring me. I hope this book has helped your journey on a path of believing, receiving and experiencing the outrageously loving gifts of God.

I would like you to have the last word in this book. Here is a space to write what you feel about actually experiencing the outcomes of your prayers. Has this experiment brought you some results to have and hold? If not yet, as sometimes it does takes time, come back to this part and write your reflections and testimonies at a later time. Receive by Faith the answers you have not yet seen.

It has been a grand pleasure to share this faith experiment with you, and I would be much obliged if any wish to share some of their writing with me as well as what took place for you in this experiment. I can be reached at fountaingateministree@gmail.com. Thank you.

1. All Quotes from the Philadelphia Gazette are found on a website called National Archives, under the heading Founder's online, with title The Kite Experiment, 19 October 1752.[https://founders.archives.gov/documents/Franklin/01-04-02-0135]

References;

Scripture quotations;

English Standard Version
ESV Bible (The Holy Bible, English Standard Version) copyright 2001 by Crossway, a publishing ministry of Good News Publishers. Used by permission. All rights reserved.
New King James Version
Copyright 1982 by Thomas Nelson. Used by permission. All rights reserved.
New American Standard Bible
Copyright 1960, 1971,1977,1995, 2020 by The Lockman Foundation. Used by permission. All rights reserved.
lockman.org
New Living Translation, copyright 1996,2004,2015,by Tyndale House Foundation, Tyndale House Publishers Inc, All rights reserved
Scripture verses were found on biblehub.com, as well as Strong's Exhaustive Concordance. Bible Hub is a most excellent website.

Other kinds of references are listed in footnotes

within the text

Printed in Great Britain
by Amazon